D1596093

PICTURING
RESTORATIVE
JUSTICE

A Vision of the World We Want to Live In.

JOAN KRESICH

ISBN 978-0-7414-7954-9
Library of Congress Control Number: 2012916228

Printed in the United States of America

Published March 2013

INFINITY PUBLISHING
1094 New DeHaven Street, Suite 100
West Conshohocken, PA 19428-2713
Toll-free (877) BUY BOOK
Local Phone (610) 941-9999
Fax (610) 941-9959
Info@buybooksontheweb.com
www.buybooksontheweb.com

"Justice is what
love looks like in public."
—Cornell West

FOREWORD

I have chosen to create a small book focused on images because of their remarkable power to penetrate the heart. Restorative justice is in a very real way a story about the human heart, about our great need to remain connected to each other, and our endless capacity for creating ways to keep our bonds with each other strong.

One very accurate way to measure our individual well-being is to look at the strength of our ties to others. Restorative justice is a tool for well-being because it works to connect and re-connect people after conflict and harm. It gets to the 'heart' of conflict and allows people to move from that heart to re-build their relationships.

This book is meant to compliment the many and varied writings on restorative justice, writings that are inspiring and directing people in communities all over the world. I hope it will find a small place among those writings, helping a new wave of people to begin the transition to restorative justice that is already underway, and making one more expression of the ancient relationship between image and word.

Joan Kresich
August 2012

WHAT IS RESTORATIVE JUSTICE?

This small book seeks to provide a rough
outline in answer to that question.

In restorative justice systems,
people come together as equals,
most often in circles
(some people call restorative justice
'circle justice')

to respond to the aftermath
of harm and painful conflict,
and to make a plan for the future
that better meets the needs of all.

In simple yet profound ways
restorative justice differs from
retributive justice.
Retributive justice is based on
punishment. Most of our responses to
harm and painful conflict are
retributive.

Reading through this book you'll
see <u>restorative justice</u>
principles and examples,
and when you turn the page,
contrasting <u>retributive</u> ones,
along with further thoughts and quotes.

Before you close the book,
you'll find a short list of resources.
You may be inspired to bring
restorative justice
to your relationships and community.

Here's a
good place
to begin...

Restorative Justice Breaks the Chain of Harms

Retributive justice adds a new harm to the chain.

My daughter made a big mistake leaving her kids alone to go to the store the night of the fire, but I can't care for them, and putting her in jail will break up our family.

"In the last three and a half decades, a new
paradigm of justice has emerged-
a justice that seeks not to punish but to heal.
A justice that is not about getting even,
but about getting well." – Fania E. Davis

"We're not talking about the scales of justice.
We are talking about a situation where
justice has occurred which has made a new
thing come to pass. A thing which leaves people
not lower, not just equal, but full and overflowing
so they can go out and spread justice to others
around them." – Dave Worth

As we break the
chain of harms,
we build peace.

Restorative Justice
Supports a Climate
of Non-Violence

Retributive justice relies on punishment. Punishment is prone to excess.

I'm joining the hunger strike. We're tired of being roughed up by guards. They broke my thumb yesterday.

"We must choose peace, because by its very nature it cannot impose itself on us."
    -James O'Dea

"If we want to reap the harvest of peace and justice in the future, we will have to sow the seeds of non-violence here and now, in the present."
    -Mairead Corrigan Maguire

"Understanding creates love, love creates patience, and patience creates unity."
    -Malcolm X

"At the center of non-violence stands the principle of love." -Dr. M L King

In order to repair harm,
we have to know
what is broken.

Restorative Justice
Looks at Harm
Through the Lens of
Human Relationships

What is broken?
Restorative justice says:

What is broken? Retributive justice says: the law, the code, the statute, the rule, the ordinance.

CA PENAL CODE 113

CITY OF SEATTLE JUST CAUSE
EVICTION ORDINANCE (SMC 22.206.160(C))

WISCONSIN EDUCATION CODE
PI 11.07 TRANSFER PUPILS

Who has been harmed? In what way?
How have relationships suffered?
Only those involved in the conflict
can answer those questions.

A law doesn't lie awake at night unable
to sleep. A statute doesn't mourn a broken
relationship. Real humans suffer
the effects of painful conflict, and they are
the ones who need to explore the meaning
that conflict has for them. Restorative
circles encourage that exploration.

We look ahead, to
create something
more beautiful.

Restorative justice
focuses on the future
and what can be done
to make things right

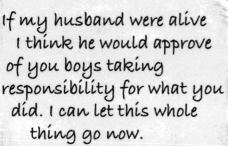

Retributive justice
searches the past
for who to blame.

"I like the dreams of the future
better than the
history of the past."
– Thomas Jefferson

Restorative justice takes us beyond
blame to a new place where we can
discover our shared fate: we are all
attempting to meet our universal
human needs—at times without
understanding the consequences
of our actions. This is our
common humanity,

What about power?
Who has it,
and how is it used?

Restorative Justice
Uses
"Power With"

Retributive justice uses "power over"

"The circle is circular not just because the chairs are arranged in a certain way, but much more profoundly because it reflects an intention to share power."
–Dominic Barter

We are moving world-wide toward the life-affirming potential of partnership systems and away from domination systems:

"The domination system supports relations of top-down rankings: man over man, man over woman, race over race, religion over religion, nation over nation, and man over nature. The partnership system supports the relations we want and urgently need at this critical juncture of history: relations of mutual respect, accountability, and benefit."
– Riane Eisler

Another look at
sharing power.

In Restorative Circles
People Come Together
as Equals

Retributive systems rely
on power hierarchies.

DEGREE
no degree

PROPERTY
no property

WEALTHY
poor

ADULT
youth

"Healing takes place
when equals meet."
-Stephen Schwartz

"When we walk into the circle our name
tags fall off. The different ways of
distinguishing human beings based on
social power are momentarily suspended
and we meet as equals. We can still
pick up our social roles, our degrees,
our street credibility, whatever we
use to distinguish ourselves from other
people, when we leave the circle."
-Dominic Barter

Who is in charge
of our response to
conflict and harm?

Restorative Justice Gives Us Control of Our Conflicts

In retributive justice the
authority determines
the scope of the conflict
and how it will be handled.

We didn't think
school suspension
would help our
son take
responsibility,
and now he's just
more angry.

"What if we were to dig to the root, Latin meaning of power, "to be able" [then] power simply means efficacy—our capacity, as philosopher Eric Fromm put it, 'to make a dent'."
— Fran Moore Lappe

"Restorative justice seeks both to reclaim and reinvigorate the role of the average citizen in achieving a sense of peace in their community and a sense of justice when that peace has been disturbed."
— James Moeser

Who is allowed
to speak and
in what way?

Restorative Justice
Supports People to
Say What They
Need to Say in
Their Own Words

Retributive systems tend to rely on legal language that limits expression.

His lawyer keeps challenging everything I say. I feel like I've been gagged.

"Congress shall make no law...
abridging the freedom of speech..."
–The Bill of Rights

"The search for truth implies a duty.
One must not conceal any part of what one
recognizes to be true." –Albert Einstein

"I Have come to believe that an as yet
undiscovered need... is the desire for
revelation." –Susan Griffin

What about neighbors,
family members,
co-workers and others
affected by the conflict?

Restorative Justice
Includes Those With
Co-Responsibilities

Retributive justice tends to limit participation.

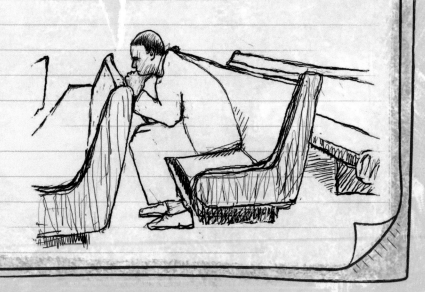

It's frustrating to sit here in the back of the courtroom. I'm his brother, and I've got important things to add, but they won't let me testify.

Conflict is often an interconnecting web, with people affecting and being affected by each other's actions.

"The conflict community is made up of people who are part of the community in which the conflict occurred, and are co-responsible for the different understandings and agreements the community has. It might be if they had a different understanding of what it means to be living together they would discover there are things they could have done to diminish the likelihood of the event ever happening." –Dominic Barter

Conflict between individuals often has its origins in larger systems.

Restorative Justice Helps People to See the Social Context for Conflict

Retributive Justice focuses on the individual.

I can't believe Rosa got fired for three tardies.

Management doesn't know the bus company dropped her bus route. Now she has to walk much further after she gets her kids off to school.

"In the land of the isolated individual, everything is privatized and public issues collapse into individual concerns so there is no way of linking private woes to social problems." –Henry Giroux

When we sit with others as equals in restorative sessions we are free to explore solutions that improve social conditions and benefit everyone.

Our limited money
doesn't have to limit
our ability to respond to
conflicts and harm.

Restorative Justice
is Affordable

The cost of lawyers and therapists is out of reach for many people and communities.

Restorative circles can be set up
using all sorts of existing spaces—
schools, churches, under-used
buildings, and park centers—making
transportation accessible and
with no cost to participants.

Making affordable responses to conflict
opens new arenas to solutions
and that in turn strengthens
the social fabric.

Creating strong
communities benefits
everyone.

Restorative Justice
Supports Those Who
Have Harmed Others
to Make Amends
and Re-Integrate
into the Community

At first we blamed you for not seeing Ernie in the crosswalk. It's lucky he wasn't really hurt. But after the circle the whole neighborhood appreciates how you take him shopping every week. He seems to love that.

Retributive justice usually ends with the punishment phase.

The people in my building don't speak to me after I got out of jail. If they don't care about me, I don't care about them.

Punishment often causes a sinkhole of anger and defensiveness, making it less likely that people will take responsibility for actions which negatively impacted others. Making amends offers a different path- a chance to transform the natural shame that results from causing harm into real accountability. This accountability represents a transformation in relationships and a hope for stronger ties in the future.

"When you walk down the street, you can look at me."
-from the film 'Burning Bridges'

Democracy—from the human heart to a world movement.

Restorative Justice Supports Authentic Democracy

In retributive systems, the authority decides the scope of individual and collective concerns.

Pollution of the schoolyard is not before the court. The only allowable issue is the legality of the protest.

Restorative justice honors the spirit of
"We the People". Restorative systems
are initiated by people, run by
people, and the solutions serve the people
who have come together.

"Is it possible to have a Democracy with
a big D in the system as a whole if you
do not have real democracy with a small
d at the level where people live,
work and raise families in their local
communities? If the answer is no, then
a necessary... condition of re-building
democracy in general is to get to
work locally." –James O'Dea

"The human heart is the first home of
democracy. It is where we first embrace our
questions: Can we be equitable? Can we
be generous? Can we listen with our
whole beings, not just our minds,
and offer attention rather than
our opinions?" -Terry Tempest Williams

RESOURCES

www.restorativecircles.org
Videos of Dominic Barter speaking, training dates, etc.

Changing Lenses: A New Focus for Crime and Justice
by Howard Zehr

The Little Book of Restorative Justice
by Howard Zehr

Nonviolent Communication: A Language of Life
by Marshall Rosenberg, Ph.D.

Living Nonviolent Communication
by Marshall Rosenberg, Ph.D

For Educators

*Discipline That Restores: Strategies To Create Respect,
Cooperation and Responsibility in the Classroom*
by Ron and Roxanne Claassen

The Little Book of Restorative Discipline for Schools
by Loraine Stutzman Amstutz and Judy H. Mullet

AFTERWORD

Both restorative and retributive justice exist on a continuum. Our responses to conflict and our systems for managing it can be more or less restorative, more or less retributive. As we reach toward restorative justice, our legal systems and the extensions of them will continue to perform important functions for us. The trend is clear though; worldwide the seeds of restorative justice are being planted in families, in communities, and in nations.

"Everything in history once it has happened looks as if it had to happen exactly that way. But I'm convinced of the uncertainty of history, of the possibility of changing what looks unchangeable." – Howard Zinn

"Look at the world around you. It may seem like an immovable, implacable place. With the slightest push- in just the right place—it can be tipped." –Malcolm Gladwell

ACKNOWLEDGMENTS

This book has its origins in the work of Brazilian Dominic Barter, who generously brings his innovations to North American trainings and workshops; in the seminal writings of Howard Zehr; in countless people in the growing international restorative justice movement who share their insights; and finally, in indigenous cultures of the world, the true originators of restorative justice, who are bringing their traditional knowledge into the glaring lights and complex problems of the present.

With gratitude to Bob, a partner in this book, and a 30 year partner in the grand and challenging work of coaxing beauty into daily life,

and to Tiny Gam, who crossed the ocean 100 years ago holding the core of her culture safely in her hands.

About the Author

Joan Kresich is an educator who has worked in schools for 35 years in general and special education. Joan brings restorative practices to her community as a practitioner and presenter. She is a climate and social justice activist, joining with others to bring about sustainable practices that nurture and protect people and ecosystems. She is also a writer and poet.
joankresich@gmail.com

About the Illustrator

R.J. Newhall's work spans the visual arts from oils and water-colors to pen & ink drawings, and ranges into wood and metal sculpture. By trade he's a fine woodworker, with a focus on creating one of a kind furniture pieces.
rjnewhall.com

About the Graphic Designer

Brad Bunkers, owner of Engine 8 Design, has over 20 years of experience in print design, brand strategy, web design, and brand identity. Bunkers is also a fine art painter and online editor.
engine8design.com